Let's go to Pentecost

Bible Stories and prayers in this book, move from Creation to Revelation to guide us through the 50 days between Easter and Pentecost.

1

Pentecost

The Israelites of the Old Testament held a Harvest Festival at the end of May to celebrate the wheat harvest, fifty days after Passover. The Jewish name for this festival is Shavnoth, meaning the Feast of Weeks. The Greek name for this festival is Pentecost meaning "fiftieth": 50 days since Jesus celebrated the Last Supper with his friends.

Praying for the coming of the Holy Spirit at Pentecost

The importance of praying together as a family has always been stressed. It is a major part of our Christian tradition.

The Church is a family which is made up from the families that are part of it together with Jesus Christ. As we pray we grow together in love for God and for one another.

"Jesus loves you.
Where does this love begin?
In your family.
How does it begin?
By praying together.
A family that prays together, stays together."
Mother Teresa of Calcutta

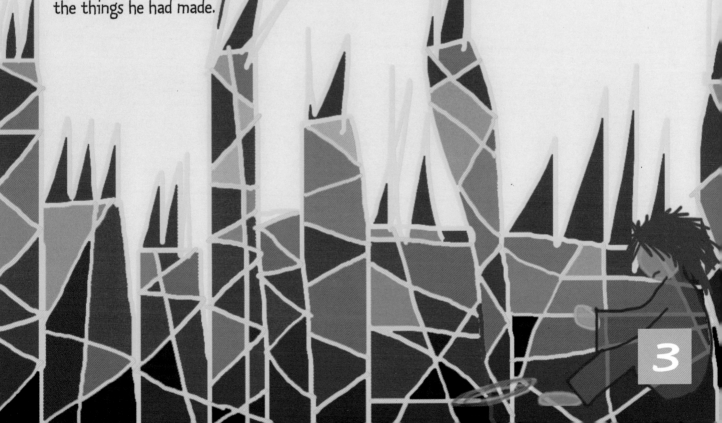

God Gets Creative

God made our world.
He had great fun making loud noises,
Bangs and explosions
As he made the stars, planets and moons.
He made the seas and the rivers,
The plants and the animals.
He made people.
Over all this he breathed his Holy Spirit like a gentle wind.
Everything was very good.
Everything made by God was filled with love from the beginning.

God made angels.
They joined him in seeing how beautiful the universe was.
They sang songs full of love and wonder to God.
But some of the angels became angry with God
And his beautiful creations.
They wanted to destroy it all.
Their leader was one of the brightest angels.
He shone before God and was called Light-bearer that is Lucifer.
But he refused to hold the Light of God any longer,
And decided to go to war against God and the other angels.
So Lucifer who is Satan gathered his army and went to war.

The very first book of the Bible tells us a story of what happenend next:
God was sad that so many had become wicked, but he continued to love
the things he had made.

3

4

He made Adam and Eve the first people and he loved them very much. God gave them a beautiful place in which to live.

"This is the Garden of Eden." He told them, "I want you to be happy here. All the food you need is here. It will always be warm enough. All the animals will be your friends, so take of it all. It is the perfect place to bring up a family, so have lots of children. It's all yours — but not the Tree in the middle. Please don't eat from that or you will be destroyed."

Adam and Eve were happy.

Satan saw this and it made him cross, so he decided to spoil it for them. In the shape of a snake he slithered into the garden where he found Eve standing near the Tree.

"The fruit on thisss Tree is the bessst." He said. "You really sshould try ssome."

"God asked us not to." Eve replied, "We might be destroyed."

"Sssilly," hissed the snake, "You won't die. You'll be wissse. You'll know everything there isss to know. Try ssome you'll ssee. Just a little bite — what harm can it do?"

What harm indeed? Thought Eve and took some of the fruit and shared it with Adam.

"It won't hurt to try a little." Said Adam.

Adam and Eve both knew that God loved them and wanted them to be happy. But they took the fruit anyway, even though they knew it was wrong, when God had asked them not to.

Later that day when God came to talk to them, they hid. They did not go to him and say sorry.

God was very sad.

"Now I have to send you away because you broke your trust." He told them. "Now you know good and bad because of the Tree. You need never have known evil."

Adam and Eve were sad now.

God sent them away but gave them his Holy Spirit to help look after them. God's world was still beautiful, but now people needed someone to help save them from all the bad things that they did.

(Genesis 1-3)

Prayers

In the name of the Father
And of the Son
And of the Holy Spirit.
                    Amen.

Dear Lord,
Thank you for making the world;
All the trees and the flowers
All the food that it gives us
All the colour and scents.
Thank you for making all the
Animals and all the people.

Help us to take care of your world.

Help us to share all the good things it gives us.
Forgive us when
we are greedy Lord,
Taking more than we should.
Forgive us when we forget to share
Or are careless with what we have.
We are sorry for all we do that makes you sad.
We are happy for all the things we do that make you glad.

Holy Spirit of God,
Guide me.
Help me do what is right.
Protect me.
Be with me each day and each night. Amen.

Now spend a couple of minutes quietly:
Imagine you are walking in the Garden of Eden.
It is full of flowers and beautiful trees. All sorts of animals peep out at you, and birds chatter and sing in the trees.
There's a little waterfall and a stream full of multicoloured rainbow fish.
Jesus comes to walk with you.
Don't say anything, just walk along quietly together looking at the garden.
Your favourite animal is there. Point it out to Jesus.
God bless the whole world. Amen.

Draw a picture of your garden of Eden

Moses and the Ark of God

All the people of Israel lived in Egypt. They had stayed there after Joseph – with his coat of many colours – had lived there.

But these days, instead of being friends with Pharaoh, they were his slaves.

Pharaoh called the people of Israel Hebrews, which means 'people over the water', because they lived on the other side of the river Nile. He was frightened of them really, and decided that if there was too many of them they might try and fight back.

To make sure nothing like that could happen Pharaoh ordered that all baby boys should be killed.

This was a terrible time.

One Hebrew woman, Jochebed had two children, Aaron and Miriam. She had another baby and it was a boy.

Not wanting to have her baby killed Jochebed made a special basket and covered it with tar so that it would float. She put her baby in the basket and sent him down river hoping that someone would see him and save him.

"Miriam." She said to her daughter. "Go and watch out for your baby brother. Pray he is rescued."

Miriam went down to the river and watched as her baby brother floated away. She prayed very hard!

Just then, Pharaoh's daughter came down to the river and seeing the basket she took the baby out of it. She had no children of her own and decided to keep this baby and she called him Moses.

When Moses grew up, God spoke to him from a burning bush.

"Moses, I want you to take the Israelites out of Egypt," said God. "Set them free. I have a new home you can take them to."

Moses had a problem with talking. He would never be able to get the words out properly. God suggested that Moses ask his brother Aaron to help. Aaron was a good brother to Moses and agreed to help.

So a couple of days later, there they both were, standing before Pharaoh asking him to let all the Israelites go free.

Pharaoh said "No!" loudly. He was angry. "I need slaves. How do you build anything without slaves? Work harder. Go away!"

God sent punishments until at last Pharaoh gave in and sent the Israelites away.

God went with them in a pillar of fire and cloud. "I will stay with you." He told them. He made sure the Egyptians could not follow and try and capture the Israelites. The Red Sea parted for Israel but quickly returned to normal, drowning all the Egyptian army that was chasing them.

The promised homeland that God had made ready was not far away.

But the Israelites would not listen to God or to Moses, and wandered around in the desert for years acting silly, sinning and hurting God. They even made a golden calf to look like an Egyptian god and worshipped that!

God was very hurt indeed. But he forgave the Israelites, and gave them ten simple rules to help them be happy.

Moses built a special Ark for God, and God lived there so that he could stay with the Israelites for as long as they wanted him.

The Ark of the Covenant – God's Promise – was the holiest place in all Israel because God lived there.

Even so, Moses had a hard time trying to keep the people from disobeying God.

At last however, despite everything, God brought the Israelites home.

With a special love, the Holy Spirit watched over God's people. No matter how much some enemies tried to hurt God's special friends, the Holy Spirit gave them the strength to carry on.

(Deuteronomy (6-7)

Prayers

Jesus, you have said "I am the bread of life. He who comes to me will never be hungry, he who believes in me will never be thirsty."
(John 6 v.35)
You give us the Bread of Life and live with us, just as you lived with the children of Israel.
Help us to remember you, because you give us so much.
Thank you for your love and kindness.

Dear Lord,
Sometimes we get lost.
We don't know what you want us to do.
Guide us Lord,
So that no matter where we are
We can always come home. Amen.

You give us many gifts.
Help us to recognise that everyone has gifts.
Do not let us see only what is wrong with people.
Moses could not speak properly
But you chose him to be one of the greatest prophets.
Teach us to respect all our neighbours and bless all those with disabilities.
Help us all to overcome our disabilities. Amen.

Spend a few minutes quietly:
Bring to Jesus all the people you know who struggle with things in life. Ask him to bless them.
Bring all those you know, friends, family and others, who do not believe in God. Ask him to bless them too.

Remember that God wants to live with you. So sit with him for a moment.
In the name of the Father and of the Son and of the Holy Spirit.

Draw a picture of a time when you got lost.

9

Jonah has a whale of a time

God needed a prophet.

He called Jonah.

"Jonah, I have a job for you," said God. "Go to Nineveh. A horrible town, and tell all the people I have seen what they are like. I have seen how they hate each other and are cruel to each other. I have seen how they have forgotten me. Tell them that in forty days I am going to let them destroy themselves."

Great, thought Jonah. It's about time someone sorted out Nineveh. Terrible place.

However as he set off on his journey, Jonah was thinking about God.

How he loves people.

How he doesn't get angry unless he has to.

How he forgives people.

"So," thought Jonah, "I'll go to Nineveh, shouting out that God will destroy them, and then he'll go all soft and forgiving! Then Nineveh doesn't get destroyed and I get to look like Jonah the Twit!"

"All aboard for Nineveh!" bellowed the captain of the nearest ship.

"Jonah the very silly twit!" thought Jonah and spun round to run to the other ship which was heading for Spain. "Viva la Jonah."

Suddenly a storm blew up, battering the ship so hard, the captain was afraid they were going to sink.

"Pray to any gods you have!" he cried to his passengers, "If you don't have a god, borrow one!"

Jonah tapped the captain on his arm. "Erm, sorry." He said, "I think this is my fault."

"What?!"

"God asked me to do something and well...I...er...ran away." He blushed. "Toss me overboard and the storm will stop."

The captain stared at Jonah. "You're a bit of a twit!" he yelled above the screaming wind.

But as the storm got worse the captain decided to try Jonah's plan, and had him thrown into the sea.

As Jonah disappeared beneath the waves, the storm stopped.

All was calm.

"Help!" thought Jonah, "God?"

A huge whale appeared and swallowed Jonah in one huge smelly gulp.

Jonah sat in the dark smelly animal for three days. On the third, it gave an almighty cough and Jonah was thrown face down onto a beach, with hard pebbles — and fresh air!

Jonah looked up and sighed. There just ahead of him, was Nineveh.

"Fine," muttered Jonah, and stomped up to the town. There, as a rather damp and fishy smelling prophet, he announced that if the people did not change their ways they would be destroyed in forty days.

The Holy Spirit entered the mind of Jonah and gave him messages from God. Out of the mouth of Jonah came the words that the Spirit wanted him to speak.

Everyone listened. They changed their ways. They began to pray and say sorry and treat each other kindly.

God was very happy and the forty days came and went, and Nineveh was not destroyed.

"What did I tell you?" said Jonah and stomped off to sulk.

It was very hot sulking.

God made a tree to give Jonah some shade while he sulked.

Then the tree died and it grew hot again.

"I liked the tree," sighed Jonah, "I'm sorry it's dead."

"I would be sorry if Nineveh and all it's people were dead," said God, "I love them."

Jonah smiled. "I know." He said. *(Jonah 1-4)*

Prayers

Dear Lord,
Help us to listen to you.
Teach us to change our bad ways and to remember you.
You do not leave us, but sometimes we leave you.
Help us to listen when you call,
Help us to do your will,
To do the things you want of us.
We ask this through Christ our Lord. Amen.

Dear Lord,
Sometimes the world seems like a terrible place.
We see wars and bad things happening.
We pray especially for . . . .
Thank you for prayer, because you have promised that it can change the world and stop wars, and bring peace.
Please send your Spirit of Forgiveness and Understanding to be with each one of us. Amen.

Dear Lord,
Just as Jonah spent three days in the darkness of the whale before bringing Nineveh back to you,
You spent three days in the darkness of death to bring the whole world back.
Thank you for all the love you show.
We are sorry when we hurt you. Amen.

Now spend some moments quietly.
If you have seen bad things on the news, or heard about them today, offer these to Jesus and ask him to help.
Imagine you are walking along the beach. You can see the fish in the water and the sun in the sky.
Jesus is walking alongside you. Ask him what he would like you to do for him.
Don't ask him for anything now. Just walk together quietly and listen.

Draw a picture of your beach

Star Light and Angels

Mary lived in Nazareth, a town in Galilee. She loved God very much and had never done anything to hurt him.

One day she sat in her little garden spinning wool, when the angel Gabriel came to see her. "Hail Mary, full of Grace," he said, "The Lord is with you."

Mary was amazed at this and a little bit frightened.

"Don't be afraid." Said the angel. "God loves you very much. He wants you to have a baby. A boy whom you will name Jesus — which means saviour. He will be the Son of God."

Mary was thoughtful. "I'm not married yet." She explained, "How will this happen?"

"The Holy Spirit will come over you." Said Gabriel, "The baby will be holy and have the title Emmanuel which means God-with-us."

Mary took a deep breath. "I belong to God." She said, "Let it be done as he asks."

Gabriel was very happy. He also told Mary that her cousin Elizabeth was going to have a baby too.

Mary immediately went to see Elizabeth who came rushing out of the house to meet her. "Blessed are you among women, and blessed is the fruit of your womb," cried Elizabeth because she was so happy about the baby Mary was going to have. The baby inside her jumped for joy,

knowing Mary and her special baby were close by.

Mary stayed with Elizabeth.

At last Elizabeth had her baby, a lovely little boy whom they named John. He was to become John the Baptist. *(Luke 1:26-56)*

Mary married Joseph, a carpenter who came from Bethlehem.

The Roman Emperor decided that everyone must sign a register in the town their family came from. So Mary and Joseph went to Bethlehem. It was there in a stable that Jesus was born. A beautiful star appeared in the sky to announce that the Light of the World had arrived.

In a nearby field shepherds were looking after their sheep. In a sudden blaze of light, a very happy angel appeared. "I have good news!" the angel announced, dancing in the sky, "The Saviour is born. The one you've been waiting for

is born in Bethlehem. You'll find him in a manger with his family around him. Go and see."
Other angels appeared then singing, "Glory to God!"
"This is great!" cried the shepherds, and the angels had barely disappeared when they were running towards the town to find the baby.
They found Mary, Joseph and Jesus, just as the angel had said. Amazed at the sight of this holy family, and that God was living with them; the shepherds knelt down and prayed.

Prayers

Let us remember what the angel Gabriel and Elizabeth said to Mary.

"Peace be with you!" The Lord is with you and has greatly blessed you··· You are the most blessed of all women, and blessed is the child you will bear."

Now say your own prayer to Mary.

Holy family, Jesus, Mary and Joseph,
Help us to pray as a family.
Mary, our Mother, you have asked us to pray as families so that we will have Peace in our homes and in our world.
We need to read the Bible to remember how much God loves us always.
Help our family to be as much like your family as we can.
So that we are patient with one another, help one another,
And always make time to be together and listen to one another.
Let us also be part of your family, so that we also make time for you. Amen.

Draw the faces of your family

colour in the disciples!

Jesus Teaches the Disciples to Pray.

Jesus had been travelling through Judea, teaching with his stories and healing many sick people. He had many friends by this time, who followed him and believed in him. He called them disciples because they were learning from him. From the many disciples Jesus had chosen twelve men to be apostles, the first leaders of his church.

One day the disciples asked him. "Jesus, will you teach us what to say when we pray? Sometimes it's difficult to know what to say to God."

Jesus smiled, "When you pray, say this;

> Our Father
> Who art in heaven
> Hallowed be thy name.
> Thy kingdom come.
> Thy will be done on earth,
> As it is in heaven.
> Give us this day, our daily bread,
> And forgive us our trespasses,
> As we forgive those who trespass against us.
> Lead us not into temptation,
> But deliver us from evil. Amen.

Jesus told them to keep on praying. The more you pray the closer to God you become.

"Ask and it will be given to you." Said Jesus, "If you look for God you will find him. If you pray God will give you what you need. If a friend asked you for a loaf of bread, you wouldn't give him a stone would you? Well, if you can be kind and generous, just imagine how generous God can be! We just have to trust in him."

Now let's spend some time looking at the prayer Jesus taught us.

Child: Our Father
Parent: God is our Father because he made us and he loves us.

Child:	Who art in heaven
Parent:	God lives in heaven first, but is with all of us, if we want him to be.
Child:	hallowed be thy name
Parent:	God's name is holy. We must never misuse his name. We must remember him with Love.
Child:	Thy Kingdom come, Thy will be done on earth
Parent:	We ask that the world will begin to see God's love so that we stop hurting one another, and the world around us. It is up to us to make a little bit of heaven on earth, by doing as God asks us.
Child:	As it is in heaven
Parent:	In heaven everyone does as God asks and are very happy.
Child:	Give us this day, our daily bread
Parent:	Let us have enough food to eat, and especially give us the Bread of Life in Holy Communion.
Child:	And forgive us our trespasses
Parent:	Forgive us when we do things that hurt you, or don't do things that would make you happy.
Child:	As we forgive those who trespass against us
Parent:	We will forgive people who hurt us, even though it can be difficult, because we need to forgive each other if there is going to be peace.
Child:	Lead us not into temptation
Parent:	Sometimes we want to do things that are wrong, perhaps because someone has asked us to, so help us not to get into those situations.
Child:	But deliver us from evil
Parent:	Protect us from bad things and making the wrong choices.
Child:	Amen
Parent:	We really mean all we say to you Lord, and want to do our best for you.

We ask all this
In the name of the Father
And of the Son
And of the Holy Spirit.
Amen.

The Last Hours of Jesus' Life

Jesus gathered his friends together for the Passover meal, when they remembered how God rescued Israel from the slavery of Pharaoh.

The twelve apostles joined Jesus for the meal. They ate specially prepared and cooked lamb with special herbs and flat bread.

Judas had already made up his mind to hand Jesus over to the Pharisees at the Temple who wanted to kill him.

When they had finished the meal Jesus took some of the bread and blessed it. Then he shared it out and said, "Take this all of you and eat it. THIS IS MY BODY."

He did the same with the wine, blessing it and giving to the apostles saying, "Take this all of you and drink it, THIS IS MY BLOOD."

This was the new promise or Covenant from God, so that sins would be forgiven, and Jesus would never leave us.

Although they knew something very special was happening, the apostles did not really understand what it was at that moment.

Jesus promised them he would send them the Holy Spirit. "The Spirit will comfort you." He said. "He will teach you many things you never knew. If ever you forget anything I told you, the Spirit will remind you." Jesus promised that the Spirit would be with them in the same way as Jesus was with them.

Afterwards they all went for a walk in a nearby garden called Gethsemane. Jesus went off alone to pray. It was terrible for him knowing that Judas was at that moment getting ready to have him arrested. He knew he was going to be killed. Worse still Jesus knew that even though he was doing this for all the people of the world, to pay for their sins, that many would not care, and would carry on hurting each other and God.

Then Judas came and the soldiers took Jesus away.

He was dragged about and shouted at. They called him names and hit him.

They took him to the Pharisees, then to Herod the King and Pilate the Roman leader.

Now that they had him Herod and Pilate did not know what to do with him.

So Pilate had him whipped and they crowned him with thorns.

Then Pilate had Jesus brought before the crowds, thinking that the sight of him battered and covered in blood would make the crowd feel sorry for him so Pilate could let him go.

But the people yelled out "Crucify him!"

So Pilate had him crucified under the title Jesus of Nazareth, King of the Jews.

Mary had seen it all. She followed her Son as he carried his cross. She felt as though her heart would break, seeing what he had to do. She was pleased when Simon of Cyrene helped Jesus.

Mary stayed with Jesus at the foot of the cross, and John one of the apostles stayed with her.

At last Jesus died and the world was plunged into darkness.

For a moment there was absolute silence. *(Mark 14:22-49, 15:1-42)*

Prayer

For a moment just sit quietly, as though you are at the foot of the cross with Mary. Sit with her and share her sadness.

When were you really sad?

. . . .

Lamb of God you take away the sins of the world
Have mercy on us and
Grant us peace. Amen.

Now spend a few minutes;
Imagine you are following Jesus as he carries his cross.
Who do you know who carries a "cross"?

. . . .

Way of the Cross:

1. Jesus is condemned to death: Pilate allows Jesus to be crucified but washes his hands to say he does not want to be responsible for deciding this.
2. Jesus is given his cross: The soldiers give Jesus the heavy cross to carry and make him walk out in front of the crowds with the two thieves carrying parts of their crosses too.
3. The cross is heavy and Jesus falls.
4. Jesus meets his Mother who is very sad.
5. The soldiers ask Simon of Cyrene to help Jesus carry the cross in case he dies before he reaches Calvary.
6. Veronica, a woman and friend of Jesus wipes his face and receives an imprint of Jesus face on her cloth.
7. Jesus falls again. It is very painful and difficult to stand up.
8. Women who are friends of Jesus and his mother are crying. Jesus tries to comfort them.
9. Jesus falls again.
10. He reaches Calvary and the soldiers strip him of his clothes.
11. They nail him to the cross.
12. Jesus dies.
13. Jesus is taken down from the cross and given to his mother.
14. They put Jesus in the tomb and seal it.
15. Three days later Jesus is risen from the dead.

Two Friends and a Stranger go to Emmaus

Three days after Jesus had been crucified, two of his friends left Jerusalem and began to walk home the few miles to Emmaus, a town nearby where they had a home.

They had heard stories that some of the women had seen Jesus alive that morning.

Confused and still very sad that Jesus had been killed, they were talking together about the awful things that had happened, when a stranger joined them.

"You look worried," said the stranger, "Is anything wrong?"

One of the men, called Cleopas, said, "You must be the only person around who doesn't know the things that have happened recently."

"What things?" asked the stranger.

Cleopas began to explain about Jesus and how he had been crucified.

He told how the sky went black and the Temple curtain had ripped in two. Many people said they saw dead people walking around.

"Now the women say they have seen Jesus alive." Cleopas shook his head. "It just isn't possible."

Then the stranger began to explain everything to them, starting with Moses and the ark and how God lived with Israel, then going through all the prophets until he spoke of Jesus and his task to save the world.

When they reached home the two friends said, "Please come in and join us. It's getting dark. We have plenty of food and room to share."

"Thank you." Said the stranger and came into the house with them.

They sat down for supper and the stranger took the bread and blessed it before sharing it out.

"Jesus!" cried both men at once. "It is you! You are alive!"

Jesus smiled and left them.

Overjoyed at what they had both seen, they immediately raced back to Jerusalem, forgetting how late it was, to tell all their friends that Jesus really is alive! *(Luke 24:13-35)*

Have you shared a special event with a friend?

. . . .

Prayers

Lord,
Let us know you
Let us invite you to share our lives with us.
Let us be silent and listen to you teach us,
through your Holy Spirit.
Fill us with your Light.
Fill us with your Love.
Fill us with your Peace. Amen.
Jesus,
You said, "I am the bread of life."
Thank you for being truly with us
Body and Blood in the signs of bread and wine.
Amen.
Spend some time quietly:
Imagine you are walking down the road towards
where you live.
Maybe you've been shopping or coming home
from work or school.
Jesus meets you and begins to walk down the
road with you.
When you reach your house invite him in. Jesus
won't come in unless you invite him. He never
forces himself on you. It's up to you.
Jesus is very happy to be invited into your home.

He loves you very much and enjoys the time he
can spend with you.
He takes a small loaf of bread and blessing it he
gives some to you.
It is the Bread of Life.

Say thank you in your own words.
Maybe there's something you would like to share
with Jesus.

. . . .

Give him a hug and show him the special things
in your house, toys and photos, maybe. Amen.

Draw some of your special things

23

Getting into the Holy Spirit of Things

After the resurrection Jesus stayed with his friends for quite a while, but then it was time to return to his Father in heaven.

"Don't worry," he said, "I won't leave you on your own. You will get help. Lots of it."

But when Jesus had gone the disciples felt afraid again and hid in the upstairs room of a house.

Suddenly the room was filled with a sound, like wind.

"What's happening?" the disciples asked one another. "A huge flame appeared hovering above their heads, and it separated into lots of smaller flames and came down on each of those in the room.

Filled with the Holy Spirit, the disciples could not wait to go out into the town and start to tell people there all about Jesus and what he had done.

They were filled with the power of the Holy Spirit and weren't afraid any more.

Peter found that when he spoke that all the people understood him no matter where they came from. Many of those listening and asking questions did not speak Peter's language, but they understood him anyway.

People were amazed not only that they understood, but at the story being told. Probably many listeners remembered Jesus being crucified and the things that had happened when he died.

"They must be drunk!" bellowed one man who was not going to accept the strange things happening around him.

"How can we be drunk?" Demanded Peter. "It's nine o'clock in the morning. We haven't had the chance to get drunk."

"Anyway, when I've had a few, I don't start speaking lots of different languages," muttered one of the crowd.

Lots of people were baptised that day from many different places. So the message of Jesus and his Church began to spread throughout the world. *(Acts 2:1-22)*

Prayers

Dear Lord,
Thank you for all the priests and ministers,
And all the people who look after us and our churches.
Thank you for all the work they do.
Bless them and take care of them.
Thank you for your special gifts so that we all have a part to play in your community.
Through Christ out Lord.
Amen.

Spend a few minutes quietly;

Thank God for the all the things he has done for the world. You have read many of them over the last few weeks.

Thank him for the special people in your life.

. . . .

Thank God for the gift of the Holy Spirit that he gave you at your Baptism.

I was baptised at . . . .

on . . . .

Thank God for the gift of the Holy Spirit that he gave you at your Baptism.
Tell God that you will spend time with him every day, so that he will always be your guide and shepherd.

25

(*The last few days before PENTECOST*)

Day 1

After receiving the Holy Spirit, the Apostles could do miracles, themselves, just as Jesus did. People were amazed and noticed how they prayed regularly together, had meals together, and shared what they had with each other. They too, wanted to become followers of Jesus. The Apostles baptised them. Those who were baptised felt the power and love of the Spirit come into them. *(Acts 2:38-43)*

PRAYER

Dear Lord,

When I was baptised, you gave me the gift of the Holy Spirit. Thank you for giving me your love then, now, and always, throughout my life. Amen.

Day 2

The Holy Spirit wanted the Apostles to preach the story of Jesus everywhere in the world. Later on, some Apostles started writing the New Testament of the Holy Bible. As Jesus promised, they were guided by the Holy Spirit. *(2 Peter 1:21)*

PRAYER

Dear Lord,

Help me to remember that whenever the Word of Jesus is spoken or read by his followers, the power of God is breathed into those words by the Holy Spirit. Amen.

Day 3

One day the Holy Spirit told Philip, the Apostle to go to a road running South out of Jerusalem. He came across a rich carriage. The man inside looked wealthy and important. He was reading the Book of Isaiah from the Old Testament, but he couldn't understand it. With the help of the Holy Spirit Philip explained the words to him and continued to tell him about Jesus. When they came to a river, the man asked to be baptised. The man continued his journey full of praise and thanking the Holy Spirit. *(Acts 8:26-40)*

PRAYER

Dear Lord,

May the Bible teach me how to love and serve God and my family and my friends. Amen.

Day 4

The Holy Spirit is love. He is the Spirit of kindness and gentleness.

Whenever we feel sorry for the wrong things we do, the Holy Spirit comes with the Spirit of forgiveness.

Whenever people get together in families or groups the Spirit comes as the bringer of unity.
(1 Corinthians, chapters 12-14)

Prayer

Dear Lord,

Thank you for working as you do in our lives and in our world. Amen.

Day 5

What does the Holy Spirit look like? He is with us today, teaching people to love and help each other. "You will recognise the Spirit," said Jesus, "for he lives inside you, and stays there." *(John 14:17)*

Prayer

Dear Lord,

Teach me to listen to the gentle voices of the Spirit when I have to make choices and difficult decisions. Let us do your will always. Amen.